DOG PARK DIARY

the social round of Goody Beagle

as "told to" Kim Pearson
photographs by Anne Lindsay

Primary Sources Books

Dog Park Diary by Kim Pearson

ISBN 978-1-932279-93-1

Photography by Anne Lindsay,
www.annelindsayphotography.com

Book design by Nancy Cleary,
www.wymacpublishing.com

Primary Sources Books
an imprint of Wyatt-MacKenzie

Primary Sources, Inc.
Issaquah, WA 98027

www.primary-sources.com

Imprint information:
www.wymacpublishing.com

Printed in the United States.

Dedication
For Ellie,
with love from Grandma and Auntie Goody

Acknowledgement
We are grateful to the dogs and their humans
who frequent Robinswood Dog Park in Bellevue,
Washington, for sharing their stories
and faces with us.

Disclaimer: Some dogs' names have been changed, and stories
altered for literary purposes. The opinions expressed herein
are the fictional opinions of Goody Beagle only and in no
way express any definitive facts.

Let Me Introduce Myself

This is me. My name is Goody Beagle.

Actually my full name is Dr. Jane Goodall Beagle. My human named me after one of her heroes.

But I'm a dog, not a hero. So no one ever calls me by my full name.

Instead they just call me Goody.

I go to the Dog Park nearly every day with my human. It's a pretty big place with trees and dirt and grass.

I don't have to wear that darn leash. I can run around and smell anything I want. The park is fenced so my human doesn't fuss over me. She doesn't have to call, "Here Goody!" just when I've found something interesting.

My Dog Park used to be a horse corral. But the horses are gone now. All that's left of them is their smell.

But hey, that's all I need!

DOG
PARK
DIARY

While I attend to my own business, my human talks with other humans. Humans are handy to have around, because they can throw balls and sometimes they have treats with them.

But I don't understand why they can't smell anything.

The smell of the Dog Park is always changing. So many dogs! I can smell that at night many other creatures visit the park. Birds and squirrels, of course. Sometimes raccoons and coyotes. And best of all - rabbits! I love rabbits!

There are many famous rabbit catchers in the Beagle Clan. Maybe someday I will be one of them.

One of the first things I do at the Dog Park is put down my own smell for the day.

Then even after I leave, my friends - and my enemies - will know that Goody Beagle was here!

Every day, I meet up with my dog friends, acquaintances, and some- times enemies at the Dog Park. I play with my friends. I ignore my acquaintances.

If any enemies come around, I show my teeth and hide under the bench my human sits on.

You can learn a lot at the Dog Park about how to get along.

That's why humans need to read this book.

Monday

Alice B. Spaniel was waiting for me outside the gate today. Her human is a friend of my human. My human writes books and her human takes pictures. The reason they are friends is they both like dogs.

Alice wanted to show off her new pink leash. When Alice was a puppy, her human put pictures of Alice on a calendar. Ever since then Alice thinks she is something special.

My leash is plain brown leather. I've never had my picture on a calendar either.

But now I have my own book!

So there, Alice.

Alice and I went inside the gate, where Barkley Lab-Spaniel and Twister Greyhound were waiting to do sniff-butt.

Barkley found out that Alice is no threat to him, so he sniffed and left. But Twister doesn't like Alice much. That's because Twister is a fashion-hound herself and thinks Alice is trying to show her up. Today Twister was wearing her red cowgirl outfit.

It's a little over the top, in my opinion.

While Twister and Barkley sniffed Alice's butt, I met up with my friend Pennylane Beagle. Even though Pennylane is from my own Clan, I still had to do sniff-butt so I would know how she was feeling today. I wouldn't want to play with her if she was in a bad mood.

Sniff-butt is the first lesson in manners for any dog. It's sort of like humans saying, "How are you?" But a lot more.

Sniff-butt lets you know who is a friend and who is an enemy, and who is feeling happy and who is feeling scared and who you should leave alone for now.

I think humans should do sniff-butt too. Maybe then they wouldn't fight so often.

They would look pretty funny, though.

Across the park, Charlie Puggle sniff-butted Kato Basenji. Charlie isn't grown up yet and hasn't learned how to interpret what he smells, so he thought Kato would play with him. But Kato is too grown up and important to play with a pup like Charlie.

The Puggle Clan is new. They are half Beagle, so I know they are at least half cool. After all, half a Beagle is better than no Beagle at all.

But their Pug half gives them a squashed-in nose. Maybe that's the reason Charlie has so much trouble with his smelling ability.

Ah, youth, so much enthusiasm! Charlie gets excited over watching the grass grow. But he will grow up eventually.

I only like puppies when they grow up to be dogs.

Over by the fence Maggie Half-Bassett and Romeo Pit-Mix were playing in a mud puddle. Maggie made the mud puddle herself. After she gets her own drink she likes to spill the rest of the water and roll in the mud she made. I don't know why.

Seems kind of selfish to me.

Romeo thought Maggie was having too much fun so he jumped on top of her. He has little-dog syndrome. Maggie is four times his size, but for some reason he thinks he can tell her what to do.

Maggie just laughs at him.

I went over to ask Punkie R. Terrier if she would like to play. At first she wasn't too sure, but I convinced her. I can be really charming if I want to be.

The Rat Terrier Clan is very fast and they like to run. They like to be in front of everyone else. Beagles like to be in back so they can chase. So Punkie and I make a good play team.

She ran around the park and I chased after her and used my special Beagle Howl. We had so much fun that other dogs wanted to join us. Sidney S. Husky cut right in front of me and I howled at him too.

This was a good way to end my Monday visit to the Dog Park.

Tuesday

Harvey Husky was in the park when I arrived today. He comes almost every day, and this makes him think he is King of the Park.

Not everyone agrees with him. Harvey has a chewed up ear

because one day one of the Rottweiler Clan thought *he* should be King instead.

But the Rottweiler got banished from the Dog Park for improper Dog Park Etiquette.

Biting is just not allowed! So Harvey is still King.

He is proud of his ear because he got it honorably in battle, just like a King should.

Actually I think his ear makes him look a little lopsided. But he can be King if he wants to be. I don't care.

DOG
PARK
DIARY

When Reagan B. Labrador came to the gate, Amber Whippet-Heeler greeted her. They were both wearing red collars. I must say those collars were quite attractive. I wear the same blue collar I've had *forever*. I wish I had a red one.

Amber and Reagan went away and played together. They didn't even ask me to come. What snobs! Well, I don't want to be friends with them anyway. Reagan tried to make up by sniffing my butt, but I told her, "too little, too late."

It's not *my* fault I don't have a stylish red collar!

Zak B. Collie tried to make friends with me, but I don't trust those herder dogs much. You never know when they're going to try to bite your heels to make you go somewhere you don't want to go. So when Amber came over to see what we were doing, I just walked away from both of them.

Walking away is so much better than fighting. The only kind of blood I like is rabbit blood.

My human thinks I don't fight because I'm a girl dog. But I think it's because I'm a sensible dog.

Or maybe only girl dogs are sensible.

DOG PARK DIARY

Amber gets very thirsty at the Dog Park because she runs after balls and sticks. She won't stop until she is so tired she falls on the ground, or her human stops throwing things, whatever comes first.

But she won't drink out of the park water dish. She will only drink from a bottle her human brings from home. Picky, picky!

I sort of agree with her about the water dish. Some dogs put their feet into the dish and make the water all muddy. I've even seen some dogs pee in the dish! (Boy dogs, of course.)

You can never be too careful, so I don't drink at the Dog Park. I wait until I get home, where I know the water is good because it comes from my human.

Barkley Lab-Spaniel is very friendly. He likes everyone.
I guess that is okay, but I think it might show a lack
of judgment. How can you like everyone? I mean, really.

Besides, he slobbers. I wish he wouldn't. He slobbers on my
head. Yuck.

Maggie Half-Bassett doesn't care about Barkley's slobber because
he tells such funny jokes. At least they are funny to Maggie.

When Casey Goldenmutt entered the park, Barkley ran right up to him and asked him to play stick. This is a game where one dog carries a stick and another dog chases him until he can take the stick away. Then they fight over the stick.

Usually only boy dogs play this game, at least for very long. Girl dogs like me get bored with it pretty fast.

Casey is almost as friendly as Barkley, but he does show some good judgment. He likes little dogs better than big ones.

He licked Manny Rat-Boston on his head to show how much he likes him.

At first Manny didn't know what to think, but he relaxed when he realized that Casey was a little dog at heart.

I have to admit I like Casey too, but I think he should leave his fleas at home.

I was happy when Ernie Beagle came to the Park. Beagles are the best Clan there is.

Casey immediately wanted to play with Ernie, and they ran around together for a while. Ernie's howl could be heard all over the park. That's okay with me, because Ernie's howl is quite beautiful. It makes me go all shivery.

But after howling and running, Ernie came back to be with me, so we could do together what Beagles do best.

Smell things!

Running and playing are good to do, but there's nothing like smelling to make you feel right with the world.

Wednesday

We were the first ones here today. I did my smell-round in peace, except for a crow who flew in and landed on the ground. I chased him, but he flew away before I could catch him and rip his feathers off. Who does he think he is, anyway? It's not the *crow* park!

A bunch of dogs showed up soon, including Alice B. Spaniel and Daisy Mae Dalmatian. Alice and I sniffed butts, because we have good manners.

Not like some. Daisy Mae Dalmatian didn't bother to sniff my butt at all, because she was in a hurry to prance around the park and let everyone admire her.

Then she rolled on the ground so Alice's human could take pictures of her.

Daisy Mae thinks she's better than everyone else, just because she is from the famous fire-fighting clan. Even though I'm sure she's never seen a fire in her life – at least one that wasn't in a fireplace.

Daisy Mae's human is a therapist and Daisy Mae is a therapy dog. This is another reason she thinks she is so cool. Just because she has a *real* job.

I bet all she does in therapy sessions is sleep or let herself be petted. Her therapeutic skills sure didn't work on Alice. Daisy Mae tried to give Alice some advice, but Alice just growled at her.

DOG PARK DIARY

Sadie and Poppy Schnauzer were eager to get into the Park. I like them because they are the size dogs are supposed to be, even though they are not beagles and cannot smell as well as I can.

Sadie is young, not quite two, and she tries to do seventeen things at once. She even tries to run and pee at the same time.

But maybe she's like that because her tail was cut off when she was a puppy, and it made her neurotic. She seems to need a lot of reassurance from her human.

Hey, maybe *I* should be a therapy dog!

DOG
PARK
DIARY

If I had my tail cut off I might be neurotic too, who knows?

But no one would cut off a Beagle's tail because that would be a great crime. Our tails are so beautiful with the little white tip on the end!

Now for a truly neurotic dog, you don't have to look much farther than Henry B. Labrador. That's his real name, but nobody calls him Henry. We all call him the Mad Pee-er.

As soon as he arrived, the Mad Pee-er ran up to my human and tried to pee on her purse, but she pushed him away in time. Then he ran over to Manny Rat-Boston and peed on his back. Then he peed on the bench, then a chair, and then a human's leg. And I lost count of how many times he peed on the fence.

Now I know that peeing is important, but enough is enough. I mean, really!

DOG
PARK
DIARY

The Mad Pee-er ran up
to Gracie P. Waterdog,
who had just come in, and
peed on her too. Gracie
barked at him, but
otherwise she didn't seem
to care.

Gracie likes to eat
flowers. She is specially
fond of dandelions.
But she's a messy eater.
Dandelion dust gets
on her beard.

I'm not sure why Gracie
comes to the Dog Park,
because she mostly just sits around. This is because
she can't go swimming here. Portuguese dogs think that
swimming is life.

So maybe she's neurotic too.

As soon as I saw Sigmund C. Terrier come in the gate, I knew I would have to leave soon. Sigmund thinks he is my boyfriend. He jumps on me every chance he gets.

Sure enough, as soon as he saw me, Sigmund came over and peed right in front of me while staring deep into my eyes. I could see that he thought this would turn me on. Of course it didn't. But he tried to climb on top of me anyway.

I growled at him but he kept on doing it. Even when I snarled, barked and tried to bite him, it didn't stop him. Sigmund is not what you'd call bright. But he is persist-ent.

Finally I had to jump on top of the picnic table to get away from him. Sigmund's legs are too short to jump up that far.

Sigmund was making such a nuisance of himself that I wasn't sorry to leave the Dog Park. Besides, some big dogs started running and barking all over the park. I do not like mob behavior. So unintelligent and unrefined! Also I am afraid I will get run over.

But I'll be back tomorrow!

Thursday

The first dog we met coming into the park was Mona Great Pyrenees MountainDog. (Her clan name is way too long, but that isn't her fault.)

Mona is a Little Dog Protector with a capital P. She makes big dogs behave. Once Mona sat on top of a Great Dane who was harassing a timid Pekinese. The Great Dane left the Pekinese alone after that. He left Mona alone too.

Everyone loves Mona. She's big, but what a softie.

I went off to smell things (a dead robin, mmm!) in the shadows behind the horse shed and came out wearing my new perfume. I think I smelled pretty good, and so did everyone else, except the humans.

But their opinion does not count when it comes to smell.

Jasper ChowMix likes to smell things too. Jasper is a loner who doesn't like to play with others. His human says she brings him to the Dog Park to "socialize" him.

I say just let him be. Not everyone has to be a social butterfly or a party animal. Some of us are the quiet kind. We are the deep thinkers of the canine world.

Or maybe I should say we are the deep *smellers*. It's the same thing anyway.

DOG
PARK
DIARY

I was happy to see Rio Y. Labrador come in. Rio is one of my favorites from the Labrador Clan. He's kind of goofy, but he has a good heart. He just wants to be your friend.

He tried to be friends with Keela Sheltie, but she ignored him. Keela looks down on goofy dogs. Yes, Keela has beautiful fur and an elegant snout. Yes, she is graceful when she runs.

But is that any reason to snub Rio?

She snubbed Henry B. Labrador too, aka The Mad Pee-er, when he tried to sniff her butt. Keela thinks her butt is too good for sniffing by mere Labradors.

DOG
PARK
DIARY

Rio doesn't need Keela's
friendship anyway. He and The
Mad Pee-er played a rousing
game of wrestle and it
seemed to make them both
very happy.

And then Tarja Plott Hound
came up and kissed him, so
his day was made! He has
lots of friends and didn't
miss Keela one bit.

Keela went and sat on a bench with Chloe Chihuahua and Chloe's human. Keela pretended not to notice when the human stroked her head.

Chloe sat on that bench for the whole hour she was at the Dog Park, most of the time huddled next to her human. Now, I know that dogs from the Chihuahua Clan are very small, but that doesn't mean they'll be mistaken for rabbits.

If they were really rabbits, then they would have something to be afraid of - me! Beagles are the best rabbit catchers in the world. And when we catch them, they're toast. Bloody mangled toast.

It makes me happy just to think about it.

Not all little dogs are like Chloe. Two of the toughest dogs I know come to my Dog Park, and they are both little dogs.

Baxter W. Corgi has a beefy body that looks way too big for his stubby little legs. But he is the most stubborn dog I've ever met and he never lets go of anything until he's darn good and ready.

Nicky J. Russell is all white except for one brown ear, and he will take on anyone he pleases.

He went right up to Barkley Lab-Spaniel and told him just what he thought of him, and believe me, what Nicky was thinking wasn't anything nice!

He went over to a group sniff-butt and tried at least ten times to sniff Twister Greyhound's butt before he finally jumped high enough to do it. Twister wasn't pleased but let him do it anyway. Nobody likes to mess with Nicky.

DOG
PARK
DIARY

Then Nicky stole a glove from
one of the humans - not even
his own human! - and wouldn't
give it back.

Instead he took it away and
played tug with it - with that
other tough little dog I told
you about, Baxter Corgi.

I don't know who won the game
of glove tug, because Baxter
and Nicky were still at it
when we had to leave.

Friday

While we were walking along the path leading to the Dog Park, Bogus B. Labrador ran up to us. He wore a collar and leash but it wasn't attached to a human. Bogus was lost.

My human took his leash and let him into the park with us, so Bogus wouldn't get in trouble with traffic. Those cars are killers, you know. I don't know why humans are so fond of them. Walking is a lot more fun.

Bogus must have been lost for a while, because the first thing he did was drink a lot of water. Very sloppily, I might add.

Bogus thought the park was great. He had never been to a Dog Park before. He chased his own shadow around and around until he got tired.

Lucky Bogus. Soon we heard a human calling, "Bogus! Bogus!" and his human came and got him. They were happy to see each other.

DOG
PARK
DIARY

As soon as Bogus and his human left, Czar Samoyed strutted into the Dog Park. Czar is a very *manly* dog. He thinks it is important that everyone knows he is the boss.

He shows his bossiness by peeing and then kicking vigorously with his back legs so dirt and grass go flying. I recommend that you don't stand in back of him when he pees. And he pees a lot!

Garfield Pitbull, another manly dog, came to the park, and he and Czar tried to out-manly each other. After they circled for a while, they peed on top of each others' pee. First Czar peed, then Garfield, then Czar, then Garfield, then Czar … Each one wanted his pee to be the top smell.

It took them a long time to run out of pee.

If it makes Czar and Garfield happy, they can pee and strut all over the Dog Park and it won't bother me one bit. It's easy to ignore them as long as you stay out of their way.

I'm glad I am a girl dog.

Sidney S. Husky galloped into the Dog Park. Sidney is big even though he is still a baby, not even six months old. He thinks he is still a little dog, so that's who he likes to play with.

He bounced right up to Skeeter Bishon and barked a giant WOOF into his face. Skeeter said Yeep! and bit Sidney on the nose. Maybe yeep is French for woof, but a bite is a bite in any language.

I felt bad for Sidney even though he's got to learn sometime. Still, who wants to have their nose bitten by a Bishon Frise?

DOG
PARK
DIARY

Crockett Mutt came to the Dog Park for the first time ever. Crockett had been abandoned by his old humans and had to live on the streets. Other dogs were mean to him and he didn't have enough to eat. This had a bad effect on his personality. He thinks everyone is out to get him.

His new humans taught him how to play ball, and now he's very good at it. Maybe this will make him easier to live with.

Ball is the favorite game at the Dog Park. Almost everybody plays, although some are better at it than others.

Tarja Plott Hound can stretch farther than anyone.

Skeeter Bishon is surprisingly good at leaping and bounding.

Lucy C. Terrier always thinks her ball is going to move on its own. She plans to pounce on it when it does. Of course, the pounce never happens because balls don't move on their own, no matter what she thinks.

Frankie C. Terrier thinks he can compete with Amber Whippet-Heeler when a human throws the ball. Amber always wins but this doesn't stop Frankie from playing.

Lucy and Frankie make me wonder about the Cairn Terrier Clan's thinking ability.

Nicky J. Russell hovers over his ball, daring a human to try to pick it up. When they do, he will snatch it and run away. He thinks this is the funniest game in the world. He'd be laughing if he didn't have a ball in his mouth.

Don't ask me what's so cool about balls. I think they are boring. Give me a rabbit any day.

While the ball players are occupied with their silly games, I have an important conference with Pennylane Beagle and Horace Harrier. A Harrier is almost as good as a Beagle – except they're just a little bit too tall. So Pennylane and I allowed Horace into our conference.

I can't tell you what was said, because it is a secret that only beagles and almost-beagles can know about.

Don't worry, our secrets aren't anything bad. We love you humans even though your smelling ability is laughable.

After we finished our meeting, we broke up for the day and went our separate ways.

Saturday

On Saturdays there are always a lot of dogs at the Dog Park. There are lots of humans too. They sit around in groups and talk to each other. Some of them laugh and tell jokes. Others complain about what bad shape the world is in. They have almost as much fun as we do.

One of the reasons humans like the dog park is that they don't have to get dressed up to come here. In fact, they seem to compete with each other for who can wear the grubbiest clothes.

Sancho G. Retriever is a friendly dog. He likes all humans, especially mine. His human tried to throw the ball for him, but Sancho preferred to play tug with my human. He wouldn't leave her alone until I reminded him that she belongs to me.

So then he went and played Frisbee with another human not his own. Maybe he's mad at his own human. I think they should make up so they can play with each other.

I don't care how friendly you are, it's not good manners to steal someone else's human.

Rex and Roxy Aussie arrived at the Dog Park together. They are littermates although Rex is mostly black and Roxy is mostly brown.

They like to bounce and push and shove and race after balls or Frisbees. Like all Aussies, they think this is the main reason for living. But they only like to play with each other. They will bark at any other dog who tries to join their game.

Rex always catches the ball while Roxy barks hysterically. Their humans call Roxy the "cheerleader."

I would call her something else if I wasn't a lady.

DOG
PARK
DIARY

I think that dogs who don't know the rules of etiquette should stay home until they learn the basics.

For instance, when a well-behaved dog has to poop, he or she will find a corner somewhere to do it. They won't poop right in the middle of a high-traffic play area.

Sophie Heeler is not a well-behaved dog. She pooped right on top of the main play hill in the middle of the park.

Luckily Sophie's human has better social skills than she does. He picked up the poop right away.

DOG PARK DIARY

Tiffany Yorkie tried to run around and smell things, but her human picked her up and sat her on the bench, whenever a dog bigger than Tiffany came too close. I think her human is afraid other dogs will eat Tiffany.

Of course, *all* dogs are bigger than Tiffany so eventually her human stuffed Tiffany inside her coat where she could be extra safe.

It's beyond me why her human brings Tiffany to the park at all.

Poor Tiffany. I hope she gets to be a real dog someday.

DOG
PARK
DIARY

With so many humans here on Saturday, it's a good day to get extra scratches and pats, and especially a good day for treats!

It's a good thing I'm not shy. I'll take loves or treats (preferably both) from anybody.

But when my own human calls for me, I am happy to go with her anywhere. Her love and treats are the best!

Sunday

On Sunday I don't go to the Dog Park. Sunday is my day to stay at home and pay attention to my human. If I don't tell her that I love her often enough, she gets cranky.

Sunday is a sitting day. We like to sit out on the porch if it is sunny. She reads a book and I let the sun soak into my fur and warm up my insides. Sometimes I close my eyes and dream about killing a nice juicy rabbit.

If it's raining we sit inside on the couch instead. Sometimes I have to sit on the floor, but only when my human is looking.

Because you can't sit all day, in the afternoon we go into the back yard. My human throws the ball for me and if I feel like it, I'll bring it back to her so she can throw it again.

But sometimes I let her get it for herself. It's good for her to move around, even on Sundays.

If I don't look out for her, who will?

My back yard is full of smells that tell me who has been trespassing on my property in the last week. You can't fool a Beagle. We can smell anything and everything.

I would make a good bomb-and-drug sniffing dog, but who wants to smell that? I like the smell of rabbits much better.

In fact, I found a place near the fence in our back yard that smelled so much like rabbits I dug a hole trying to find them.

I would have found them, too, but my human told me to stop digging holes. So the rabbits got away this time.

I have a great life!

I live with a good human, even though her nose
is really pitiful.

I have good food to eat
and a warm place to sleep
at night.

I have lots of friends,
who I get to see every day
at the Dog Park, where
there's always something
going on.

And I have a few small
enemies, just enough to
make life spicy.

What more could a Beagle want?

Except maybe a rabbit or two once in a while.

About The Author

Kim Pearson is an author, ghostwriter, teacher, and the owner of Primary Sources, a writing service that helps others communicate their stories, histories and ideas. In addition to *Dog Park Diary: the Social Round of Goody Beagle*, she is the author of non-fiction books *Making History: How to remember, record, interpret and share the events of your life* and *You Can Be an Author, Even if You're Not a Writer*; and fiction *Eating Mythos Soup*, *Common Disguises*, and *Animal ABC*. She has also ghostwritten more than thirty non-fiction books and memoirs. Kim lives near Seattle, Washington, with her cat Morgan and her opinionated dog, Goody Beagle. More about Kim and the services of Primary Sources can be found on www.primary-sources.com.

About the Photographer

Anne Lindsay is an award-winning photographer who creates images for authors, books, and magazines on location and in her studio nestled on the banks of a lake. In addition to *Dog Park Diary: the Social Round of Goody Beagle*, she photo-illustrated *Before It Wriggles Away* by children's author Janet Wong. Anne lives near Seattle, Washington with her husband Frank, her daughter Fiona, and their dog Alice B. Spaniel. More about Anne and her services can be found on www.annelindsayphotography.com.

About the Book Designer

Nancy Cleary is an award-winning graphic designer who launched an independent press to empower women writers. She lives and works near the beautiful Oregon coast in Deadwood, with her office dog, Book C. Labrador, her son Wyatt, daughter MacKenzie, the kids' dad Joey, and his dog, Truck B. Labrador.